cooking with

AVOCADOS

Elizabeth Nyland

The Countryman Press
Woodstock, VT
www.countrymanpress.com

Interior photographs by the author unless otherwise specified
Book design and composition by Nancy Freeborn

Published by The Countryman Press, P.O. Box 748, Woodstock, VT 05091
Distributed by W. W. Norton & Company, Inc., 500 Fifth Avenue, New York, NY 10110
Printed in the United States of America

Cooking with Avocados
978-1-58157-251-3

10 9 8 7 6 5 4 3 2

For Adrian, Cohen, and Isla. You are the reason I started on this amazing journey of healthy cooking; you inspire me every day to find new and exciting things to cook and eat.

Contents

Preface

If you have picked up this book, even to browse, then I can safely assume that you dig avocados. For a large part of my life, the only time I ever consumed avocados (or alligator pears, as they are also known) was in the well-known and ubiquitous dip known as guacamole. For years, I had no idea that there was much you could do with avocados, beyond mashing them and dipping things into their fatty flesh. In fact, my father often quoted his own mother, who told him in the '50s that avocados were very fattening and should not be eaten too often. She went so far as to write "300" on the bumpy skin, to remark on its high calorie content. While it's true that avocados can be high in fat and calories, they should not be looked at as something to avoid. (More detail on the health benefits of avocados and avocado oil can be found on page xv.)

In 2009, when I started my food blog, *Guilty Kitchen*, I often used avocados as a topping, in dips and dressings, and as a garnish for Mexican-themed entrées. As the years went on, my creativity surrounding this amazing fruit began to truly blossom. I give full credit to the wonders of food blogging for my interest in new and exciting things to do with avocados. When you have readers waiting for you to create recipes and leaning on you for knowledge, you begin to really delve deep into creativity.

I started to find out about using avocados to replace other fats in baking or in recipes that might usually involve sweeter fruits. I made a green pie. I freaked out about how good it was. I made more green things. I got my kids to grow their own avocado plants so we could have a little piece of the tropics right here in our northern climate.

My experiments paid off and this book was born. I truly hope it will inspire the creative chef in everyone by reshaping the way we think about a humble fruit we've come to take for granted.

Introduction

This book is about more than just avocados being mashed and used as dips. This book is here to highlight the true versatility that avocados can offer. A slightly underripe avocado can taste refreshing, juicy, and light while a very ripe avocado will be heavy and smooth and have a fatty mouthfeel. With this knowledge, I created a cookbook to showcase the truly amazing tropical fruit we have all come to recognize.

The recipes in *Cooking with Avocados* are intended to be easy and approachable, with easy-to-find ingredients and simple techniques. As in my previous book, *Cooking with Coconut Oil*, I have tried to cover every meal of the day, with desserts and snacks added for good measure. In *Cooking with Avocados*, you'll find many of your favorites (like guacamole and salsa) with a little twist or personal touch that I've come to love over the years. You'll also find more off-the-wall recipes like Avocado Pancakes, Savory Oatmeal, and Mini Avocado Cheesecakes. These recipes were designed to light a spark in you to really push your cooking comfort zone. Not everyone will look at an avocado smoothie and say, "Yum!" but once you try it, I promise you that it will change your mind. I hope this book opens your eyes to the wonder that is the avocado.

Avocado How-Tos

Select a dark green (not black) avocado. Do not try to squeeze it to see how ripe it is, as this bruises the soft flesh underneath and leads to those ugly brown spots in the flesh. Instead, pick up a dark green specimen and gently push the stem to the side. Below the stem should be a vibrant green color. If it is brown or pale, it is either over-ripe or underripe. If you are buying many avocados at once, choose a bag of bright green avocados and allow them to ripen at room temperature until the above is true.

HOW TO PIT AN AVOCADO

Pitting an avocado is quite easy if you know what to do. Done with care and safety, removing the pit is a walk in the park. Follow my step-by-step photos opposite to pit like a pro!

1. Slide your knife into the flesh and cut all the way around (lengthwise is the best option), trying to finish at the place where you began. Make sure the knife reaches all the way to the pit. Then twist the halves apart, exposing the pit.

2. Whack the pit with the sharp edge of the knife blade, embedding the blade in the pit. Then turn the knife 90 degrees, freeing the pit from the flesh.

3. Depending on the recipe, you can cut the avocado into cubes with the point of a knife while it is still in the skin and then scoop out the flesh with a spoon or, for perfect slices, peel the skin off the whole half and slice the avocado on a cutting board.

HOW TO KEEP AN AVOCADO FROM BROWNING

Keeping avocados from browning may be one of those mysteries of the universe people are always trying to solve. Do you leave the pit in? Cover it in plastic, tinfoil or wax paper? Do you salt it or not? Squeeze citrus juice all over it?

I've tried all of these methods and none of them works. But I have stumbled upon a method that works 100 percent of the time and will keep your avocado from browning for up to 24 hours. This method works best with larger sections of avocado that still have the skin on them. Small pieces of avocado will absorb more water and should not be left in the soak for more than a few hours.

Here are the three easy steps:

1. Fill a small bowl with room-temperature water.

2. Stir in 1 teaspoon of sea salt until dissolved.

3. Place the cut avocado in the bowl, keeping the flesh side down (skin side up), cover, and refrigerate until needed (up to 24 hours).

Health Benefits of Avocados and Avocado Oil

Avocados and their oil are full of monounsaturated fat, which can help reduce low-density lipoprotein (LDL) cholesterol (the bad one) while possibly raising high-density lipoprotein (HDL) cholesterol.

- They may reduce the risk of metabolic syndrome, thereby reducing the risk for diabetes, stroke, and heart disease.
- They are high in phytochemicals, which may help prevent certain types of cancer.
- They can increase absorption of other nutrients such as carotenoids, which are fat-soluble. A high level of the carotenoid lutein is known to protect against age-related macular degeneration.
- They are anti-inflammatory because they contain phytosterols, antioxidants, omega-3 fatty acids, and polyhydroxylated fatty alcohols.
- They contain high levels of potassium, which helps control blood pressure.
- They are rich in folate, a B vitamin that is essential in preventing birth defects such as neural tube defects and spina bifida.

Breakfast

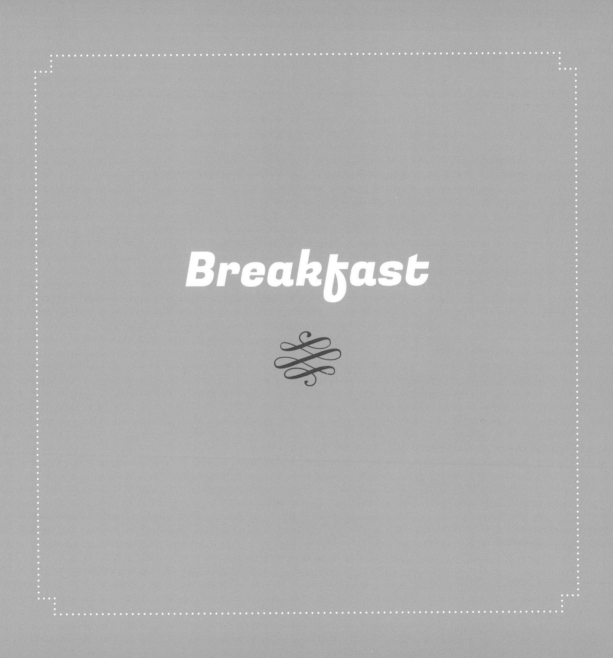

Avocado and Mango Smoothie

If you're a fan of avocados, you have probably seen them paired with mangoes at least once. They make a beautifully complex and flavorful duo and are quite colorful together in salads or salsas (like the Mango and Avocado Salsa on page 23). In this refreshing smoothie, the avocado creates a smooth and creamy texture along with the Greek yogurt, and the mango gives a tropical sweetness that is perfect for breakfast, snacks, or meals on the run.

YIELD: 1 SERVING

⅔ cup unsweetened almond milk or other nondairy milk

1 mango, peeled and pitted

½ large avocado

⅓ cup plain nonfat Greek yogurt

1 Tbsp honey

1 tsp vanilla extract

Pinch ground cinnamon (optional)

4 or 5 ice cubes

Place all the ingredients in a blender in the order listed and process in short bursts until the ice has been thoroughly crushed. Continue to process until smooth, 10 to 15 seconds. Serve.

Chocolate-Banana Smoothie

Chocolate and banana are an age-old flavor combination, but add the creaminess of avocado and you have one mind-blowing superfood smoothie! To create the perfect creamy smoothie, freeze the banana a day in advance; this makes a big difference in the end result. Of course, in a pinch, a room-temperature banana will work, but freezing the banana gives this smoothie a milkshake-like consistency.

YIELD: 1 SERVING

¾ cup unsweetened almond milk or other nondairy milk

½ small avocado

½ small banana, frozen

1 Tbsp cocoa powder

2 very soft medjool dates, pitted

5 or 6 ice cubes

Place all the ingredients in a blender in the order listed and process in short bursts until the ice has been thoroughly crushed. Continue to process until smooth, 10 to 15 seconds. Serve.

Lime and Avocado Smoothie

Smoothies are a fantastic way to fit in a meal when you are in a rush in the morning, during work, or when you just don't have time to sit down to eat. Mixing the creamy, satisfying flesh of avocado with a good amount of carbohydrates (from the banana) makes for a lasting "full" feeling. If you plan on eating this as more than just a snack, add a scoop of protein powder for a more well-rounded meal.

YIELD: 1 SERVING

¾ cup unsweetened almond milk or other nondairy milk

½ small avocado

2 tsp honey

½ large banana, preferably frozen

1 Tbsp lime juice

4 or 5 ice cubes

Place all the ingredients in a blender in the order listed and process in short bursts until the ice has been thoroughly crushed. Continue to process until smooth, 10 to 15 seconds. Serve.

Avocado Pancakes

As pancakes go, these are one of my kids' favorites. They come out light and fluffy, like a pancake should, but contain none of the not-so-great ingredients of a regular old Sunday-morning pancake. These pancakes are grain-, gluten-, dairy-, and soy-free and are as versatile as any other. Stud with chocolate chips, blueberries, bananas, or whatever else your family loves. They freeze well and are perfect reheated in the toaster.

YIELD: 6 LARGE PANCAKES

½ cup pureed avocado (about ¾ large avocado)

4 pastured eggs

2 Tbsp maple syrup

1 Tbsp vanilla extract

½ tsp apple cider vinegar

3 Tbsp coconut flour

2 Tbsp ground golden flaxseeds

1 tsp baking powder

½ tsp ground cinnamon

¼ tsp sea salt

1. In a medium bowl, whisk the avocado, eggs, maple syrup, vanilla, and vinegar together.

2. In a second bowl, stir together the coconut flour, flax, baking powder, cinnamon, and salt.

3. Pour the wet ingredients into the dry and stir to combine.

4. Heat a large nonstick frying pan over medium heat. Pour the batter into the desired size and cook for 1 to 2 minutes per side. (Bubbles will form on the surface when it is time to flip the pancakes.)

5. Serve immediately, or cool on a wire rack. Freeze flat for easy reheating.

Bacon and Egg Cups with Avocado

Bacon and eggs are a classic breakfast staple in North America, though this meal has a bad reputation because of its saturated fat content. I'm on the "saturated fat is good for you" bandwagon, and our family enjoys a good bacon and egg breakfast on a regular basis. Sometimes, though, you have to switch it up to keep everyone interested in it because, yes, even bacon can get old. These little cups were inspired by the "cured meat in muffin tins" trend that has been popular online over the years. Adding the avocado before cooking does change the flavor and texture slightly, but our family loves it. It's like finding a little treasure at the bottom of your breakfast.

YIELD: 2 SERVINGS

Butter or coconut oil

4 slices thick-cut bacon

½ large avocado, diced

4 pastured eggs

Sea salt and fresh-cracked pepper

1. Preheat the oven to 375°F. Lightly grease four cups in a muffin tin with butter or coconut oil.

2. In a large, heavy-bottomed frying pan, cook the bacon over medium-low heat until lightly cooked, but still pliable, 3 to 4 minutes.

3. Divide the diced avocado evenly among the greased muffin cups.

4. Line the sides of each muffin cup with a slice of bacon. Crack an egg into each muffin cup and season with salt and pepper to taste. Bake for 15 to 20 minutes or until the whites are firm and the yolks are still slightly soft.

5. Cool the bacon and egg cups in the muffin tin for 2 to 3 minutes, then carefully remove them from the tin by running a rubber spatula around the edges of each one. Serve immediately.

Mushroom, Brie, and Avocado Omelet

One of my absolute favorite breakfast foods is an omelet dripping with gooey Brie and wilty spinach. Paired with savory mushrooms and the bright flavor of avocados, this omelet has topped my favorites list for the better part of a decade. I simply cannot find a better combo than what is in this omelet. I often serve these as dinner in our house, paired with steamed vegetables or roasted potatoes, because what is better than breakfast for dinner?

YIELD: 1 SERVING

1 tsp butter

1 cup white or cremini mushrooms
    (7 or 8 mushrooms), chopped

1 cup greens (such as arugula, spinach,
    Swiss chard, or kale), chopped

1 ounce Brie cheese, sliced

3 pastured eggs

Sea salt and fresh-cracked pepper

2 tsp pesto or Avocado Pesto Cream (page 53)

¼–½ small avocado, sliced

1. In a small nonstick frying pan, heat the butter over medium heat. Add the mushrooms and cook until softened. Add the greens and cook until soft, about 5 minutes. Season with salt and pepper if desired and transfer to a small bowl; do not wash the pan.

2. Beat the eggs in a bowl with salt and pepper until fluffy.

3. Heat the empty pan over medium-low heat. Add the beaten eggs and cook for about 4 minutes or until the eggs are thickened but still slightly wet on top.

4. Arrange the slices of Brie evenly across one half of the omelet. Top with the cooked mushroom-spinach mixture and the pesto. Using a spatula, fold the empty side of the omelet over the filled side. Continue to cook until the Brie begins to melt, about 2 minutes.

5. Top the omelet with the avocado slices and serve immediately.

Sausage and Sweet Potato Hash

Sausage and potato hash is usually served as a brunch item and sometimes comes with a fried egg on top or smothered in cheese, depending on where you are. Here, the hash is topped with the bright and refreshing notes of avocado for a pleasant palate pleaser (try saying that three times fast!). Serve this for dinner along with a green salad or for brunch with eggs served any which way you like (fried eggs cooked soft make a nice stand-in for gravy).

YIELD: 4 SERVINGS

1 Tbsp plus 1 tsp melted coconut oil

1 lb sweet potatoes, peeled and diced

Sea salt and fresh-cracked pepper

1 sweet or yellow onion, diced

4 large bratwurst or other pork sausages, chopped into bite-sized pieces

2 large, firm apples (such as Gala, Fuji, or Granny Smith), peeled, cored, and diced

½ tsp dried thyme or 1 tsp fresh

½ tsp dried sage or 1 tsp fresh

1 large avocado, halved, pitted, and diced

1. Preheat the oven to 400°F. In a large bowl, toss the potatoes with 1 tablespoon of the oil and salt and pepper to taste. Pour the potatoes onto a parchment paper–lined baking sheet. Roast until soft and slightly browned around the edges, about 30 minutes.

2. Meanwhile, in a large, heavy-bottomed frying pan or Dutch oven, melt the remaining 1 teaspoon oil over medium heat. Add the onion and cook until browned, 10 to 15 minutes. Add the sausage, apples, thyme, and sage and cook for 10 to 15 minutes more.

3. Toss the onion mixture with the potatoes, top with the avocado, and serve.

Savory Oatmeal

Oatmeal in North America is usually full of sugar and all sorts of other unhealthy ingredients; plus, it's usually poured from a packet and cooked in a microwave. I'm here to tell you right now, though, that oatmeal is one of the easiest things to make on this planet and it is exceptionally satisfying when it's made with a savory slant. For a filling and long-lasting breakfast, adding a bit of protein is always a good idea. Here, a fried egg, butter, and avocado make for a satisfying meal.

YIELD: 1 SERVING

1 cup water

¼ tsp sea salt

½ cup old-fashioned rolled oats

1 pastured egg

2 tsp butter

¼ large avocado, sliced

1. In a small saucepan, bring the water and salt to a boil over medium heat.

2. Add the oats, lower the heat, and simmer, stirring occasionally, for 10 minutes.

3. While the oats are cooking, melt the butter in a small frying pan over medium-high heat.

4. Crack the egg into the butter and fry until the desired doneness is reached, 2 to 3 minutes for soft, 3 to 4 minutes for medium, or 5 minutes for hard.

5. Spoon the oatmeal into a bowl and top with the egg and the remaining butter from the pan. Lay the sliced avocado on top and serve immediately.

Appetizers, Snacks, and Dips

Avocado and Cucumber Soup

This chilled soup is ideal for hot summer days when you just do not want to turn on the oven or cook something on the stove. The refreshing flavors of cucumber, basil, and lemon marry with the creamy flesh of the avocado for a perfect appetizer for your summer gathering. Garnish with a drizzle of crème fraîche or a dollop of plain yogurt and a pinch of chopped chives. Bellissimo!

YIELD: 6–8 SMALL SERVINGS (3 CUPS)

½ large English cucumber, peeled and
    cut into chunks

1 avocado, halved, pitted, and peeled

1 cup cold water

½ cup canned full-fat coconut milk

1 tsp grated lemon zest plus 3 Tbsp lemon juice

2 Tbsp lime juice

2 Tbsp minced fresh chives

1 Tbsp chopped fresh basil

¼–½ tsp sea salt

1. Place all the ingredients in a blender and process until smooth.

2. Transfer to a bowl, cover, and refrigerate until ready to serve. (This soup is best if made the same day you are serving it.)

Avocado Salsa, Three Ways

Avocado lends itself very well to being mixed with the normal salsa ingredients, but it also makes quite a statement as the star of fruit salsas and other alternatives. Here the avocado is paired with black beans and corn for a Southwest feel, mangoes for a sweeter approach, and cilantro, lime, and tomatoes for that good old-fashioned salsa my mother taught me how to make. Bring all three to get-togethers for a real treat or make any one for those Mexican nights at home. Adjust the amount of jalapeño to your tastes. For mild salsa, use ¼ to ½ jalapeño; for medium salsa, use ½ to 1 whole; and for very spicy salsa, use the whole chile, including the seeds.

MANGO AND AVOCADO SALSA

YIELD: 1½ CUPS

½ large avocado, diced
1 small mango, peeled, pitted, and diced
1 Tbsp lime juice
Sea salt
1 Tbsp chopped fresh cilantro
¼–1 jalapeño, seeded and finely chopped

Mix all the ingredients together in a bowl and serve immediately.

SOUTHWEST SALSA

YIELD: 1½ CUPS

½ large avocado, diced
½ cup canned black beans, drained and rinsed
½ cup frozen corn kernels, thawed*
Sea salt
1 Tbsp chopped fresh cilantro
1 Tbsp lime juice
¼–1 jalapeño, seeded and finely chopped

Mix all the ingredients together in a bowl and serve immediately.

Note: To use fresh corn, bring a pot of water to a boil. Add one ear of corn, remove from the heat, and let stand for 10 minutes. Drain and cool. Remove the kernels with a sharp knife.

ZESTY SALSA

YIELD: 1½ CUPS

½ large avocado, diced
1 tomato, seeded and diced
1 Tbsp chopped fresh cilantro
1 tsp grated lime zest plus 1Tbsp lime juice
½ small sweet onion, finely diced
¼–1 jalapeño, seeded and finely chopped

Mix all the ingredients together in a bowl and serve immediately.

Avocado Tzatziki

Traditional Greek tzatziki is always made with thick and creamy Greek yogurt (never sour cream), a touch of dill, and sometimes a squeeze of lemon. In this variation, the dense and creamy avocado replaces some of the yogurt to make a delightfully green dip or spread. Serve this tzatziki with grilled chicken or pork, or take it to your next potluck—it's delightful served with pita bread or chips for dipping.

YIELD: 1½ CUPS

1 large avocado, halved, pitted, and peeled

½ cup plain nonfat Greek yogurt

3 Tbsp lemon juice

½ clove garlic, minced or grated

½ English cucumber

1 Tbsp extra-virgin olive oil

½ tsp dried dill

¼ tsp sea salt

Fresh-cracked pepper

1. Process the avocado, yogurt, lemon juice, and garlic in a blender or food processor until smooth. Transfer to a bowl.

2. Grate the cucumber, then put in a fine-mesh strainer and press on it to squeeze out the excess liquid.

3. Add the drained cucumber, oil, dill, salt, and pepper to taste to the avocado mixture and stir to combine. Serve or cover and refrigerate until needed.

Caramelized Onion Dip

Onion dips at parties are often made with dried soup mix and other mysterious ingredients. Try making your own from scratch with this very simple recipe. The flavors of real caramelized onions far surpass those of the dried soup kind and, when mixed with creamy avocado and plain nonfat Greek yogurt, make for a much healthier alternative. It's perfect with chips, crackers, or cheeses.

YIELD: 2 CUPS

2 tsp coconut oil, tallow, butter, or lard

1 large sweet onion, diced

½ tsp sea salt

1 Tbsp chopped fresh thyme

1 large avocado, halved, pitted, and peeled

3 Tbsp plain nonfat Greek yogurt

2 tsp red wine vinegar

1. In a large, heavy-bottomed frying pan, melt the oil over medium heat. Add the onion and cook, stirring occasionally, until very deep brown and quite soft, 15 to 20 minutes. Add the thyme and salt, remove from the heat, and cool to room temperature.

2. Process the avocado in a blender or food processor until very smooth, scraping down the sides as needed. Add the yogurt and vinegar and process to blend.

3. Once the onions has cooled to room temperature, stir together with the avocado puree and place in a serving bowl. Serve immediately or cover and refrigerate until needed.

Green Hummus

Hummus is a traditional Middle Eastern dish made from cooked, mashed chickpeas usually blended with tahini, olive oil, lemon, salt, and garlic. The word hummus actually means "chickpeas" in Arabic. These days with every kind of hummus under the sun being made, it's no surprise that it would show up here, mixed with the smooth flesh of avocados. Together they make a very creamy and dense dip, perfect for vegetables, chips, or flatbreads.

YIELD: 1½ CUPS

1 (14-oz) can chickpeas, drained and rinsed
½ large avocado
3 Tbsp extra-virgin olive oil
3 Tbsp lemon juice
2 tsp tahini (sesame seed paste)
1 small clove garlic, minced or grated
½ tsp sea salt
Paprika (optional)

1. Process the chickpeas, avocado, 2 tablespoons of the oil, the lemon juice, tahini, garlic, and salt in a blender or food processor until very smooth, scraping down the sides of the bowl as needed.

2. Transfer to a bowl and garnish with the remaining 1 tablespoon oil and the paprika (if using). Serve immediately or cover and refrigerate until needed.

Mango and Avocado Skewers with Honeyed Yogurt

This is a very simple recipe that takes about 10 minutes to make, including mixing the dip and cutting the fruit. It's perfect for brunches with friends or after-school snacks (it's fancy enough for kids to be interested in helping make and eat it). If it's summer, feel free to add pieces of strawberry or pineapple—the flavors go together exceptionally well. For this recipe, choose a relatively firm avocado, as the cubes will remain firmly on the skewers and the fresh flavor will better match the soft and juicy mango.

YIELD: 4 SKEWERS

2 large mangoes, peeled, pitted, and cut into bite-sized cubes

1 large, firm avocado, halved, pitted, and cut into bite-sized cubes

⅓ cup heavy cream

1 Tbsp honey

1 tsp vanilla extract

⅓ cup plain nonfat Greek yogurt

2 tsp lime juice

1. Skewer the avocado and mango cubes through their centers, alternating between the two, until each skewer is three-quarters full.

2. In a large bowl, whip the heavy cream with the honey and vanilla until thick. In a small bowl, stir together the yogurt and lime juice.

3. Fold the yogurt mixture into the whipped cream and place in a small serving bowl. Serve immediately alongside the skewers or cover and refrigerate until needed.

Nori-Wrapped Avocado with Toasted Sesame Sauce

The star of this show is the sauce! This creamy, salty, sesame-spiked sauce is often served accompanying steaks in Japanese teppanyaki restaurants. Dipping the cold wedges of avocado into this sauce is pure heaven. Serve this dish before a meal of sushi or rice-based dishes so you can use up the remaining sauce on your entrée. Serve this appetizer immediately after you make it, because the avocado may brown if left out too long.

YIELD: 8 SMALL SERVINGS

Toasted Sesame Sauce

3 Tbsp diced sweet onion

3 Tbsp heavy cream

2½ Tbsp sesame seeds, toasted in a dry pan until light brown

1 pastured egg yolk

½ clove garlic, grated (optional)

3 Tbsp tamari

3 Tbsp avocado oil or extra-virgin olive oil

Avocados and Nori

2 nori sheets, each cut into 8 strips

2 large avocados, halved, pitted, and each half cut into 4 wedges

1. For the toasted sesame sauce: Process the onion, cream, sesame seeds, egg yolk, and garlic (if using) in a blender or food processor until smooth.

2. Add the tamari and oil and process for 10 to 15 seconds.

3. Pour into a container, cover, and refrigerate until needed.

4. For the avocados and nori: Fill a small bowl with water. Wrap a strip of nori around an avocado wedge, wetting the ends of the nori with water so that they will stick together. Repeat with the remaining nori and avocado. Serve immediately with the sesame sauce.

Perfect Guacamole

For years, my parents have traveled to the Baja Peninsula every fall and returned rested, relaxed, and full of stories in the spring. They always bring back Mexican ingredients that can't be found in grocery stores here, along with advice on how to use them. I've always made guacamole, but it has since been refined to an authentic version after asking my mother what she gets down on the beaches of Ensenada. This recipe has no garlic (traditional Mexican guacamole doesn't use garlic) but the jalapeño and cilantro give it lots of flavor. If you can get them, use Key limes or Mexican limes for the lime juice, but they are small so make sure to buy a few. If you're not fond of spicy food, use the smaller amount of jalapeño or leave it out altogether.

YIELD: ABOUT 1 CUP

1 large avocado, halved, pitted, and peeled

1 small Roma/plum tomato or 4 or 5 cherry tomatoes, chopped

¼ sweet onion, finely diced

2–3 Tbsp chopped fresh cilantro

¼–1 jalapeño, seeded and finely chopped

1 Tbsp lime juice

½ tsp sea salt

In a large bowl, mash the avocado until it is just slightly chunky. Add the tomato, onion, cilantro, jalapeño, lime juice, and salt and stir to combine. Serve.

Shrimp Salad Rolls

I've been making variations of these salad rolls since the very first days of my blog, *Guilty Kitchen*. They are simple, filling, delicious, and have endless filling possibilities. You can fill these with just about anything and they will be amazing and impressive to all your dinner guests. I usually stick to Asian themes, as I love the flavor of ginger and garlic with the avocado and rice noodles. The textures all work well together, but if you need more crunch, try raw grated carrot, chopped raw cabbage, or matchstick cucumbers. Serve these with soy sauce for dipping or with Toasted Sesame Sauce (page 32).

YIELD: 8 ROLLS

1 lb large shrimp or prawns, peeled and deveined

4 oz rice noodles (vermicelli)

3 Tbsp tamari

2 Tbsp rice vinegar

2 Tbsp sesame oil

1 Tbsp honey

1 Tbsp chopped fresh basil

1 Tbsp chopped fresh cilantro

2 tsp fish sauce

1 tsp grated fresh ginger

4 green onions, sliced lengthwise into strips

½ small yellow bell pepper, sliced into strips

8 rice paper wraps

8 leaves red or green leaf lettuce

1 avocado, halved, pitted, and thinly sliced

1. Bring a large pot of water to a boil, add the shrimp, and remove from the heat. Let stand for 2 to 3 minutes. Drain the shrimp and rinse immediately under very cold water. Slice each shrimp in half lengthwise and set aside

2. Fill the same pot with water again, bring to a boil over high heat and add the noodles. Boil for 2 minutes, drain, and rinse with cold water. Drain again and set aside in a large bowl.

3. In a small bowl, mix together the tamari, vinegar, oil, honey, basil, cilantro, fish sauce, and ginger. Toss the sauce with the noodles, then add the green onions and yellow pepper and toss to combine.

4. To prepare the wraps, fill a bowl with hot water (just cool enough to touch). Dip a rice paper wrap into the water, then transfer to a moist tea towel to soak up the excess liquid. Lay a lettuce leaf on the wrap and fill with one-eighth of the noodle mixture. Place 2 to 4 shrimp halves on top and finish with a slice or two of avocado, then roll up by folding the bottom edge toward the top, then the two sides in towards the middle, then roll up and place on a plate seam side down. Repeat with the remaining wraps, then serve.

Prosciutto-Wrapped Avocado

Prosciutto is one of my very favorite cured meats. It comes from the dry-cured hind leg of pigs or boars and is usually served raw (called *prosciutto crudo* in Italian). Its salty, savory flavor is perfect for pairing with sweet and creamy textures. I have often served prosciutto-wrapped fresh figs stuffed with goat cheese and grilled on the barbecue to great delight from my dinner guests. Here the prosciutto is paired with refreshing slices of avocado and drizzled with a sweet melon and balsamic sauce. You'll need 16 slices of prosciutto for this recipe. Slices of prosciutto vary in size depending on how you buy them; you can cut larger slices into smaller pieces if necessary to get the right number.

YIELD: 16 SERVINGS

¼ honeydew or cantaloupe melon, peeled and
    sliced (about 1½ cups or 4 ounces)
2 Tbsp aged balsamic vinegar
5 ounces thinly sliced prosciutto
2 avocados, halved, pitted, and each half cut
    into 4 wedges

1. Process the melon and vinegar in a blender or food processor until completely smooth.

2. Gently wrap a slice of prosciutto around each avocado wedge and lay on a platter or individual plates.

3. Drizzle the melon sauce over the wrapped avocado wedges and serve immediately.

Smoky Chipotle Cheese Dip

Chipotle chiles are simply jalapeños that have been smoked and dried, giving them an earthy, slightly sweet spiciness. Blended with cream cheese and avocado, they make a dip that is intricately layered in flavor and is perfect for dipping vegetables, chips, or flat breads.

YIELD: 2 CUPS

8 ounces cream cheese

1 large avocado, halved, pitted, and peeled

2 Tbsp finely chopped canned or jarred chipotles in adobo sauce

½ tsp sea salt

½ tsp ground cumin

½ tsp garlic powder

Process all the ingredients in a blender or food processor until smooth. Transfer to a bowl, cover, and refrigerate until ready to serve. (The dip will keep for up to 24 hours.)

Zucchini Tuna Boats

Lunches can get pretty boring if all you ever eat are leftovers, sandwiches, or takeout. Tuna can be overlooked for many reasons, not least of which is the memory of being forced to eat your mom's tuna fish sandwiches every day as a youngster. These awesome zucchini boats not only reinvent tuna for lunch but they also appeal to a wide crowd. They are gluten-, grain-, dairy-, and egg-free but still fill you up and taste great. Prepare the night before for a perfect no-utensils-needed lunch.

YIELD: 2–4 SERVINGS

½ large avocado

2 Tbsp plain nonfat Greek yogurt

1½–2 Tbsp lemon juice

1 Tbsp chopped fresh basil

2 tsp Dijon mustard

½ tsp sea salt

Fresh-cracked pepper

1 large zucchini (about 8 inches long)

1 (6-oz) can pole-and-line-caught yellowfin or albacore tuna, drained

2 green onions, chopped

1 small Roma/plum tomato, chopped

1. Process the avocado, yogurt, lemon juice, basil, mustard, salt, and pepper to taste in a blender or food processor until smooth.

2. Cut off the ends of the zucchini, and then slice in half lengthwise. (For four small servings, slice each half crosswise.) Scoop out the middle flesh, keeping about ¼ inch of flesh on the "boats." Chop the scooped-out flesh into bite-sized pieces and set aside in a medium bowl.

3. Add the tuna, half of the green onions, tomato, and avocado sauce to the chopped zucchini and stir to combine.

4. Spoon the filling into the boats, top with the remaining green onions, and serve.

Salads and Dressings

Avocado-Lemon Dressing

This light and refreshing dressing works well for salads or as a dip for vegetable platters. Change the flavor profile by choosing the ground cumin or the fresh basil; both work quite well.

YIELD: 1¾ CUPS

1 large avocado, halved, pitted, and peeled

⅓ cup finely diced red or sweet white onion

⅓ cup plain nonfat Greek yogurt

2 tsp grated lemon zest plus 3 Tbsp lemon juice

2 Tbsp apple cider vinegar

½ tsp ground cumin or 2 Tbsp finely chopped
   fresh basil

2 tsp honey

¼ tsp sea salt

Fresh-cracked pepper

1. Process the avocado and onion in a blender or food processor until smooth. Add the yogurt, lemon zest and juice, vinegar, cumin (or basil), honey, salt, and pepper to taste and process to blend.

2. Store in an airtight container in the refrigerator until ready to serve. (The dressing will keep for up to 24 hours.)

Peach, Avocado, and Basil Dressing

This dressing is thick, sweet, and vibrantly flavored with the spiciness of fresh basil. It lends itself well to chopped salads, pasta salads, or as a dip for vegetables and also makes a fantastic sauce for roasted chicken. Try tossing it with your favorite summer salads for that perfect hint of sweet and savory.

YIELD: 1 CUP

½ ripe peach, skin on

¼ cup loosely packed fresh basil

½ avocado

2 Tbsp apple cider vinegar

2 Tbsp aged balsamic vinegar

Sea salt

1. Process all the ingredients in a blender or food processor until smooth, scraping down the sides of the bowl as needed.

2. Store in an airtight container in the refrigerator until ready to serve. (The dressing will keep for up to 2 days.)

Avocado Mayonnaise

Making mayonnaise at home can be difficult. Sometimes the emulsion breaks when the oil is added, making for a huge headache if you don't know how to save it. Replacing the egg or egg yolks with avocado is the perfect way to make "foolproof" mayonnaise. This mayonnaise does not break easily and tastes almost exactly like true mayonnaise. Besides being impossibly easy, this recipe is also vegan!

YIELD: 1½ CUPS

1 large avocado, halved, pitted, and peeled (about 1 cup flesh)
1–2 Tbsp lemon juice
2 tsp Dijon mustard
½ tsp sea salt
⅓ cup avocado oil or extra-virgin olive oil

1. Process the avocado, lemon juice, mustard, and salt in a blender or food processor on low speed until very smooth. Scrape down the sides as needed.

2. Increase the speed to medium-low and slowly drizzle in the oil as the blender runs. (The oil should form a very thin stream; do not pour it in faster or you will risk "breaking" the mayonnaise.) Continue until all the oil has been added. Store in an airtight container in the refrigerator until ready to serve. (The mayonnaise will keep for up to 3 days.)

Avocado Pesto Cream

Pesto is such a rich and sumptuous sauce. It can be made in many ways to fit dietary restrictions but usually contains a couple of basic elements. Most pesto is made with copious amounts of basil and olive oil and also traditionally contains garlic, pine nuts, and Parmigiano-Reggiano. I have seen kale pesto, pesto with walnuts, sun-dried tomato pesto, and even blueberry pesto. This version uses avocado to make the traditional sauce even creamier. It's perfect for burgers.

YIELD: 1 CUP

1 cup loosely packed fresh basil

1 small avocado, halved, pitted, and peeled

¼ cup extra-virgin olive oil

3 Tbsp raw hemp hearts

3 Tbsp nutritional yeast or Parmesan cheese

½ clove garlic, minced or grated

½ tsp sea salt

1. Process all the ingredients in a blender or food processor until completely smooth, scraping down the sides of the bowl as needed.

2. Transfer to an airtight container and store in the refrigerator until ready to serve. (The pesto will keep for up to 3 days. If you want to store it longer, pour a layer of olive oil to completely cover the top; this keeps oxygen from getting to the pesto and causing it to turn brown. Use within 6 days.)

Avocado and Broccoli Salad

Some friends of ours brought a raw broccoli salad over to our house one night for a get-together and we all fell in love. It was simple, traveled well and tasted amazing. After thinking over the combinations that would work well with the broccoli, I settled on this iteration. The creamy avocado contrasts with the crispy, salty bacon and the tart lemon does the same with the sweet cherry tomatoes, making for a dish perfect for parties. It pairs well with chicken, fish, or pork and keeps well in the refrigerator overnight.

YIELD: 4–6 SERVINGS

3 slices thick-cut bacon

½ large avocado

1 tsp grated lemon zest plus 4 tsp lemon juice

½ cup plain nonfat Greek yogurt

2 tsp Dijon mustard

¼–½ tsp sea salt

1 lb broccoli, cut into very small florets (3 cups)

¾ cup cherry tomatoes, halved

½ small red onion, finely diced

1. In a large, heavy-bottomed frying pan, cook the bacon over medium heat until crisp. Set aside on a paper towel–lined plate.

2. Process the avocado, lemon zest and juice, yogurt, mustard, and sea salt in a blender or food processor until smooth.

3. In a large bowl, combine the broccoli, tomatoes, and onion. Pour the avocado dressing over the vegetables and toss to combine. Crumble the bacon and sprinkle over the salad. Serve immediately or refrigerate until needed.

Avocado Coleslaw

Coleslaw is notorious for being an overly dressed and very unhealthy salad. Using avocado-based mayonnaise makes for a light and refreshing version of this barbecue classic. This very basic coleslaw recipe can be added to in various ways. Try cilantro and a touch of sesame oil for an Asian kick, apples sliced into matchsticks for a sweet crunch, purple cabbage for a touch of color, or even chopped up veggies like tomatoes, bell peppers, or whatever's handy.

YIELD: 4–6 SERVINGS

½ head green cabbage, shredded

2 medium carrots, peeled and grated

4 green onions, chopped

¾ cup Avocado Mayonnaise (page 50)

¼ cup unsweetened almond milk, milk, or buttermilk

2 Tbsp apple cider vinegar

½ tsp dry mustard

Sea salt and fresh-cracked pepper

Black sesame seeds (optional)

1. In a large bowl, mix the cabbage, carrots, and green onions together.

2. In a small bowl, whisk together the mayonnaise, milk, vinegar, mustard, and salt and pepper to taste. Pour over the vegetables and toss to combine.

3. Garnish with sesame seeds (if using) and serve immediately.

Potato Salad

It's not quite a summer barbecue without the inevitable potato salad drowning in bottled mayonnaise and paprika. Change it up a little by using avocado-based mayonnaise and grainy Dijon mustard for a tangy, creamy, but healthy version of this family favorite. Because there are no eggs used in the mayonnaise, this salad can sit out on your picnic table with no worries while you attempt to relearn the magical art of the Frisbee.

YIELD: 4 CUPS

4 large russet potatoes (about 1¾ lb), peeled
    and cut into 1-inch cubes
½ cup Avocado Mayonnaise (page 50)
2 Tbsp extra-virgin olive oil
2 tsp grainy Dijon mustard
1 tsp apple cider vinegar
½ tsp paprika
¼ tsp sea salt
¼ cup chopped green onions

1. Place the potatoes in a large saucepan and cover with water by 2 inches. Bring to a boil over high heat, then lower the heat and simmer for 20 minutes. Drain the potatoes, then transfer to a large bowl and cool to room temperature.

2. In a small bowl, whisk together the mayonnaise, oil, mustard, vinegar, paprika, and salt. Pour the dressing over the cooled potatoes and stir to combine. Sprinkle the green onions on top and refrigerate until ready to serve. Stir the green onions into the salad before serving.

Chicken Salad

Chicken salad is an old favorite, but it's often made with leftover bits of chicken no one seems to pay attention to until they are mixed with mayonnaise and slapped on some bread. Liven up this classic salad by instead mixing the chicken with avocado, Greek yogurt, and refreshing lemon. Served on bread, in lettuce cups, or even by itself, it makes for a satisfying and healthy lunch that is easily packed for work or school.

YIELD: 2–4 SERVINGS

1 lb boneless, skinless chicken thighs or breasts

Sea salt and fresh-cracked pepper

½ large avocado

⅓ cup plain nonfat Greek yogurt

1 tsp grated lemon zest plus 1½ Tbsp lemon juice

1 celery stalk, chopped

¼ cup chopped green onions

1. Season the chicken with salt and pepper. Heat a large, heavy-bottomed nonstick frying pan over medium heat and add the chicken in a single layer. Cook for 10 to 15 minutes, turning once or twice, until cooked through. Transfer the chicken to a plate and chill in the refrigerator until cold (about 1 hour).

2. Meanwhile, process the avocado, yogurt, lemon zest and juice in a blender or food processor until smooth. Stir in the celery and green onions and season with salt and pepper to taste.

3. Chop the cooled chicken into bite-sized pieces and stir in the dressing. Serve immediately or store in an airtight container in the refrigerator for up to 3 days.

Cobb Salad

Cobb salad is one of my favorite salads. There is so much going on in this salad that it seems more like a regular meal than a salad. The greens are really just a plate to hold all the goodness. Make sure you choose the very best ingredients, as each one is the star of its own little show. The fun here is in the plating. Pile each ingredient up in its own place and you have a very fun meal for two!

YIELD: 2 SERVINGS

Salad

2 pastured eggs, room temperature

1 tsp avocado oil

2 boneless, skinless chicken breasts

Sea salt and fresh-cracked pepper

4 slices thick-cut bacon

5–6 cups organic spring mix

12 cherry tomatoes, halved or quartered

1 large avocado, halved, pitted, and sliced

4 oz fresh goat cheese, crumbled

Vinaigrette

¼ cup plain nonfat Greek yogurt

2 Tbsp avocado oil or extra-virgin olive oil

1 Tbsp aged balsamic vinegar

2 tsp Dijon mustard

1. For the salad: Preheat the oven to 375°F. Line a baking sheet with aluminum foil and brush lightly with the avocado oil. Place the chicken on the sheet, season with salt and pepper as desired and cook for 25 minutes. Remove from the oven and slice or chop.

2. While the chicken is cooking, place the eggs in a small saucepan, cover with cold water, and bring to a boil over high heat. Cover the pan and let sit off the heat for 10 minutes. Remove the eggs from the hot water and run under cold water for a few minutes. Set aside.

3. In a large, heavy-bottomed frying pan, cook the bacon over medium heat until crisp. Set aside on a paper towel–lined plate and crumble when cool.

4. Arrange the greens on two plates. Arrange the tomatoes, bacon, avocado, cheese, and chicken on the greens. Peel and slice the hard-boiled eggs and place them where desired.

5. For the vinaigrette: Whisk all the ingredients together and pour over the salad. Serve.

Crab Salad

Living on the West Coast my entire life, I've been exposed to many fresh seafood delicacies that may not be available in other parts of the world. One example is Dungeness crab, an abundant crustacean that lives only on the West Coast of North America. The flesh is delicate and sweet, and if pressed, I would choose it every time over lobster. If you are not as lucky as I am, choose good-quality canned crab that has at least 25 percent claw meat. Serve this salad with crackers or small pieces of toast, or as a sandwich filling.

YIELD: 4 SERVINGS

½ large avocado

2 Tbsp heavy cream

2 Tbsp plain nonfat Greek yogurt

1–2 Tbsp lemon juice

2 tsp Dijon mustard

½ tsp sea salt

Fresh-cracked pepper

6 oz fresh crabmeat, cooked, or canned
    crabmeat, drained

¼ cup chopped green onions

1. Process the avocado, cream, yogurt, lemon juice, mustard, salt, and pepper to taste in a blender or food processor until very smooth.

2. In a small bowl, stir the crabmeat with the avocado mixture and top with the green onions. Serve.

Egg Salad

Egg salad is often branded as very unhealthy because of its high saturated fat and calorie content. Mixed with store-bought mayonnaise and served on white bread, egg salad may deserve that reputation. Next time you find yourself craving this classic dish, try making this healthy version and serve it in lettuce wraps or on sprouted-grain bread.

YIELD: 4 SERVINGS

6 pastured eggs

1 large avocado, halved, pitted, and peeled

2 tsp red wine vinegar

2 tsp Dijon mustard

1 tsp paprika (optional)

½ tsp sea salt

Fresh-cracked pepper

¼ cup chopped green onions

1. Place the eggs in a small saucepan, cover with cold water, and bring to a boil over high heat. Cover the pan and let sit off the heat for 12 minutes. Remove the eggs from the hot water and run under cold water for a few minutes. Set aside until cool, then peel and chop.

2. In a bowl, mash the avocado with a fork and stir in the vinegar, mustard, paprika (if using), salt, and pepper to taste.

3. Mix the avocado with the eggs (you may not need all of the avocado mixture) and top with the green onions. If using in sandwiches or wraps, stir the green onions into the salad. Serve.

Grapefruit and Avocado Salad with Poppy Seed Dressing

In this salad, the sharp and bitter notes of the grapefruit are complemented by the smooth and creamy avocado and a sweet-tart dressing. This salad is beautiful in hot summer months and pairs extremely well with seafood and chicken. Prepare the dressing in advance (up to 24 hours) and make the rest of the salad just before serving. If you don't enjoy the bitterness of grapefruit, this salad also works quite well with navel oranges.

YIELD: 4 SERVINGS

Dressing

½ cup plain nonfat Greek yogurt

1 tsp grated lemon zest plus 3 Tbsp lemon juice

2 Tbsp avocado oil or extra-virgin olive oil

1 Tbsp honey

1 Tbsp poppy seeds

¼ tsp sea salt

Salad

2 large grapefruits

4 cups mixed baby greens

1 large avocado, halved, pitted, and sliced lengthwise

1. For the dressing: Whisk all the ingredients together until smooth.

2. For the salad: With a small, sharp knife, slice off the top and bottom of a grapefruit, to remove the peel. Place the grapefruit on a cutting board and cut off all the peel, following the shape of the fruit. Slide the knife along one membrane that separates the section of fruit and cut the fruit from the membrane, then do the same on the other side to free the section of fruit. Repeat for the remaining sections, then peel and section the second grapefruit the same way.

3. Place the greens on small plates, top with the grapefruit sections and avocado slices, drizzle with the dressing, and serve.

Jicama, Bacon, and Avocado Salad

Jicama, or Mexican yam (as it's sometimes called), is a crunchy, starchy tuber with a slightly sweet flavor. It is perfect grated in salads or alone with a squeeze of lime and a sprinkle of salt, but also does well in many kinds of recipes. Because of its crunch and sweet flavor, it pairs well with sour, bitter, and creamy ingredients. Here, the jicama is paired with creamy mashed avocado and the salty crunch of bacon. It's a perfect replacement for potato salad if you are looking for something a little lighter and a little more exciting.

YIELD: 4 SERVINGS

Sea salt

1 large jicama

5 slices thick-cut bacon

¼ cup plain nonfat Greek yogurt

1 Tbsp avocado oil

2 tsp Dijon mustard

⅓ cup chopped green onions

½ large avocado, cut into 1-inch cubes

1. Fill a medium bowl with room-temperature water and stir 1 teaspoon of salt into the water. Using a sharp knife, cut the top and bottom off the jicama. Rest the jicama cut side down on a cutting board and slide the knife from top to bottom to remove the thick skin. Cut the jicama into bite-sized cubes and place in the water (this prevents the jicama from browning and adds a bit of flavor).

2. In a large, heavy-bottomed frying pan set over medium heat, cook the bacon until crisp. Set aside on a paper towel–lined plate.

3. In a small bowl, whisk together the yogurt, avocado oil, mustard, and salt and pepper to taste.

4. Drain the jicama and place in a serving bowl. Add the green onions and avocado and toss together. Pour the dressing over the vegetables and stir to combine. Crumble the bacon over the salad and serve. (The salad can be stored in an airtight container in the refrigerator for up to 2 days.)

Mango and Avocado Rice Salad

Mango and avocado are so good together, they should probably get married already! The sweet and firm flesh of the mango is the perfect accompaniment to the soft, buttery avocado, and with the addition of the rice and basil, you have a very bright and refreshing side dish to pair with fish, poultry, or pork.

YIELD: 4 SERVINGS

1½ cups water

1 cup jasmine rice

2 tsp coconut oil

¼ tsp sea salt

2 Tbsp avocado oil or extra-virgin olive oil

1 Tbsp chopped fresh basil

1 Tbsp lime juice

2 tsp honey

1 small mango, peeled, pitted, and cut into
   ¾-inch cubes

½ small avocado, cut into ¾-inch cubes

1. In a small saucepan, combine the water, rice, coconut oil, and salt. Bring to a boil over high heat, lower the heat, cover, and simmer for 15 minutes. Remove from the heat and let stand, covered, for 10 minutes.

2. While the rice cooks, mix the avocado oil, basil, lime juice, and honey together in a small bowl.

3. Transfer the rice to a medium bowl, add the mango, avocado, and dressing, and toss to combine. Serve warm.

Pear and Avocado Salad

At first, pear and avocado may not seem like a good pairing, but once you've tasted a juicy Bartlett pear next to the smooth flesh of avocado, you'll change your mind. This salad is perfect as an appetizer or served alongside chicken or fish. It has a light, mild flavor and is perfect for those hot summer days. Try it with a sweet white wine for an extra-special meal.

YIELD: 4 SERVINGS

2 large ripe Bartlett pears

1 large avocado, halved, pitted, and peeled

3 Tbsp plain nonfat Greek yogurt

1 Tbsp lime juice

1 Tbsp honey

1. Slice the pears in half lengthwise, then into quarters. Carve out the seeds and then slice the pears into ¼-inch-thick half-moons. Slice the avocado into similar-sized pieces.

2. Arrange the pear and avocado slices in an alternating pattern on four plates.

3. In a small bowl, whisk the yogurt, lime juice, and honey together. Drizzle over the salads and serve.

Sides

Oil-Mashed Potatoes

Mashed potatoes are a mainstay of any good family gathering, but are generally reserved for special occasions because they are usually mixed with copious amounts of butter and cream and/or topped with gravy. Here, the potatoes are mixed with avocado oil and light cream to make perfectly fluffy, light-as-air mashed potatoes. They are great on their own (I like them topped with a little truffle salt), drizzled with gravy, or used as a base for potato pancakes.

YIELD: 6–8 SERVINGS

4 large russet potatoes, peeled and cut into
    1-inch cubes

1 tsp sea salt

2 Tbsp avocado oil

3 Tbsp light cream or half-and-half

1. Place the potatoes in a large saucepan, cover with water by 2 inches, and stir in ½ teaspoon of the salt. Bring to a boil over high heat, then lower the heat and simmer for 20 to 25 minutes or until the potatoes are tender. (Poke with a small paring knife; if the knife meets little to no resistance, they are done.)

2. Drain the potatoes and return them to the pot. Add the oil and mash with a potato masher. When thoroughly mashed, add the cream and remaining ½ teaspoon salt and mash until completely mixed. Serve immediately.

Herb-Roasted Potatoes

Most recipes for roasted potatoes involve olive oil, refined vegetable oils, or animal fats, but here they are paired with highly adaptable avocado oil. The simple, clean flavors of the potatoes are accented with fresh herbs and earthy garlic. For the best flavor and texture, I always use new (or nugget) potatoes; my favorites are fingerlings, Yukon Golds, and German Butterballs. Pair this classic dish with grilled or roasted meats, simple vegetables, or salad.

YIELD: 4–6 SERVINGS

2 lb new potatoes

2 Tbsp avocado oil

Coarse sea salt and fresh-cracked pepper

3 cloves garlic, peeled and lightly smashed

2 sprigs fresh rosemary

2 sprigs fresh thyme

2 sprigs fresh sage

1. Preheat the oven to 375°F.

2. Cut the potatoes into 1-inch pieces (quarters or halves, depending on how big they are). Place in a 9 x 13-inch glass or metal baking dish. Pour the oil over the potatoes, season with salt and pepper to taste, and stir to coat.

3. Scatter the garlic and herb sprigs over the potatoes. Roast for 45 to 50 minutes or until the potatoes are slightly golden brown and crisp on the bottom. Serve.

Quinoa with Kale, Avocado, Cilantro, and Bacon

Quinoa (KEEN-wah) is a versatile seed (not a grain), closely related to spinach and beets. It is gluten-free and easy to prepare, which has led to a surge in its popularity over the last decade. Higher in protein than brown rice, quinoa is also high in calcium, dietary fiber, and iron. Quinoa is also high in saponin, a bitter-tasting glycoside, which to some can be a gut irritant. Always rinse your quinoa two or three times before cooking to make sure you remove as much of the saponin as possible.

YIELD: 6–8 SERVINGS

1 cup quinoa

2 cups water

½ tsp salt

3 slices thick-cut bacon, chopped

6 large kale leaves, stemmed and roughly chopped

Sea salt and fresh-cracked pepper

1 large avocado, diced

2 Tbsp chopped fresh cilantro

1. In a fine sieve, rinse the quinoa until the water runs clear. Drain and place in a medium saucepan with the water and salt. Bring to a boil over high heat, then cover, lower the heat, and simmer for 15 minutes. Remove from the heat and let stand, covered, for 10 minutes.

2. In a large, heavy-bottomed frying pan, cook the bacon over medium heat for about 5 minutes. Add the chopped kale and cook 5 to 7 minutes longer. Season with salt and pepper to taste.

3. Mix the kale-bacon mixture with the cooked quinoa and place in a serving bowl. For a warm dish, top with the avocado and cilantro and serve. For a cold salad, refrigerate the mixture for 2 hours or more, then stir, top with the avocado and cilantro, and serve.

Sautéed Mixed Vegetables

For this recipe, I chose a few of my favorite colorful and nutritious veggies to showcase the versatility of avocado oil. This dish is perfect to accompany grilled, roasted, or fried meats or for filling fajitas and wraps. Replace the dried herbs with fresh herbs (in the same quantities), add garlic if desired, or top with a drizzle of good-quality aged balsamic vinegar for a more Italian flavor.

YIELD: 4–6 SERVINGS

1 Tbsp avocado oil

8 oz white or cremini mushrooms, thinly sliced

1 large onion, thinly sliced

1 large yellow bell pepper, stemmed, seeded, and
   sliced into thin strips

1 large red bell pepper, stemmed, seeded, and
   sliced into thin strips

2 small or 1 medium zucchini, sliced into thin strips

1 tsp dried basil or oregano

Sea salt and fresh-cracked pepper

1. In a large Dutch oven or cast-iron frying pan, heat the oil over medium heat. Add the mushrooms and onion and cook until browned, 10 to 15 minutes.

2. Add the bell pepper, zucchini, and basil and season with salt and pepper to taste. Continue to cook until the vegetables are softened but still have a slight crunch (al dente), 7 to 8 minutes. Serve immediately.

Shrimp and Avocado–Stuffed Tomatoes

These tomatoes are perfect for a first course at a multicourse dinner, as a side dish to accompany lighter dishes or even on their own as a light lunch. Use the very best quality tomatoes you can find (local heirloom varieties usually have the most flavor) and don't skimp on the shrimp, either. I prefer small West Coast shrimp from local waters, as they are sweet and flavorful, but large shrimp chopped up will work just fine, too.

YIELD: 4 SERVINGS

4 medium tomatoes

1 large avocado, halved, pitted, and diced

10 oz cooked and peeled small shrimp

¼ cup Avocado Mayonnaise (page 50)

1 tsp grated lemon zest plus 3 Tbsp lemon juice

Sea salt and fresh-cracked pepper

1. Using a sharp paring knife, core the tomatoes. Scoop out the seeds and soft membranes. Set aside.

2. In a medium bowl, combine the avocado, shrimp, mayonnaise, lemon zest and juice, and salt and pepper to taste.

3. Scoop the salad mixture into the tomatoes and serve immediately.

Shrimp-Stuffed Avocado with Bocconcini

Stuffing avocados is a given, at least to me. Once you remove the pit, there is a convenient little bowl to pack deliciousness right into. In this simple, fast, and healthy salad, shrimp is paired with small, sweet tomatoes and sweet and creamy baby bocconcini. Bocconcini are small balls of mild un-ripened mozzarella (which is traditionally made with water buffalo milk). They are packaged in whey or water and are widely available. If it's the height of summer when you make this dish, feel free to add a couple of leaves of fresh basil, torn into small pieces. You'll fall in love with the classic flavors of Caprese salad all over again.

YIELD: 2 SERVINGS

1 large avocado

1½ Tbsp lemon juice

Sea salt and fresh-cracked pepper

8 oz cooked and peeled small shrimp

7 or 8 cherry tomatoes, halved (¼ cup)

¼ cup mini bocconcini, (7 or 8 "pearls")

1. Cut the avocado in half and remove the pit. Scoop out some of the flesh from each half, leaving about ½ inch of flesh on the skin.

2. Place the scooped-out flesh in a bowl with the lemon juice and salt and pepper to taste, and mash until slightly chunky.

3. Mix the shrimp, halved tomatoes, and bocconcini into the avocado mash and scoop back into the avocado halves. Serve immediately.

Mains

Avocado-Stuffed Meatballs

Meatballs are a favorite in our house, simply because they are a simple, quick meal to make that the kids love. They are perfect for little hands to pick up without the need for utensils and also delicious in many kinds of sauces. My kids will even eat them cold the next day for lunch! You may think stuffing them would be difficult, but the secret is to use a very small amount. Be careful when folding over the edges to seal up the meatball, as the filling can seep out a bit. For an exotic flair, try using a tablespoon of minced preserved lemon rind in place of the lemon zest and juice.

YIELD: 12 OR 13 MEATBALLS

1½ lb lean ground grass-fed beef

1 lb lean ground pastured pork

3 Tbsp chopped sun-dried tomatoes

1 Tbsp grainy Dijon mustard

1 tsp dried basil

1¼ tsp sea salt

1 tsp grated lemon zest plus 1½ Tbsp lemon juice

1 large avocado, halved, pitted, and peeled

2 tsp coconut oil

1. Preheat the oven to 400°F. In a large bowl, combine the beef, pork, tomatoes, mustard, basil, 1 teaspoon of the salt, and the lemon zest.

2. In a separate bowl, mash the avocado, then add the lemon juice and remaining ¼ teaspoon salt and stir to combine.

3. Form the meat mixture into small (golf ball–size) balls with your hands and, working with one at a time, create a divot in the center to form a sort of hollow cup. The meat should be about ¼ inch thick. Fill the center with about 1 teaspoon of the avocado mixture and then carefully pinch the edges around to seal it in. (You may need to add a tiny piece of the ground meat mixture to seal it up tight; you don't want any of it escaping during the cooking process.)

4. In a large, heavy-bottomed frying pan, heat the oil over medium heat. Add the meatballs and cook until slightly browned on all sides, 1 to 2 minutes. Transfer the browned meatballs to a baking sheet and cook in the oven for 10 to 15 minutes. Serve immediately.

Pan-Fried Steak with Avocado Compound Butter

Steak can be overwhelming to some novice cooks. The thought of cooking a piece of meat to everyone's desired "doneness" can be nerve-wracking. What if you overcook your beautiful $10 grass-fed strip loin? Not to worry. The very first thing to do is to learn to cook a steak in a frying pan where it is a lot easier (most of the time) to control the temperature of the cooking surface. Barbecues tend to have hot spots and can lead to charred edges and overcooked meat. Try this method the next time you want a simple steak, or in the depths of winter, when outdoor grilling is the last thing on your mind.

YIELD: 2 SERVINGS

2 grass-fed strip loin steaks about 1 inch thick, trimmed, room temperature

Sea salt and fresh-cracked pepper

2 tsp salted butter

2 (¼-inch-thick) slices Avocado Compound Butter (recipe follows)

1. Heat a large cast-iron frying pan over medium-high heat until a drop of water dripped into the pan sizzles and evaporates. Season the steaks on both sides with salt and pepper to taste.

2. Melt the salted butter in the pan. Add the steaks and cook on one side for 3 to 4 minutes. Flip once with tongs (not a fork!) and cook for 3 to 4 minutes. (This is for rare. Add a minute or so per side for medium-rare.)

3. Set the steaks on serving plates and top each with 1 slice of the compound butter. Allow to rest for 2 minutes and serve.

Notes: For medium or well-done steak, cook over lower heat so that the outside of the steak does not burn while the inside cooks. Do not cover the steak while cooking. If your steak is extremely thick, after searing it on the stove, finish the steak in the oven at 350°F until the desired doneness is achieved.

AVOCADO COMPOUND BUTTER

Compound butters are ubiquitous in French cuisine and are often served at steak houses in the form of parsley and garlic butter. Here avocado and butter are blended together with a hint of lemon and coriander. Perfect with steak, it is also quite complementary to fish, chicken, and vegetables.

YIELD: ABOUT 1 CUP

1 large avocado, halved, pitted, and peeled
¼ cup salted butter, softened
1 tsp grated lemon zest plus 3 Tbsp lemon juice
½ tsp ground coriander

1. Process all the ingredients in a blender or food processor until smooth. Scrape down the sides as needed.

2. Lay a sheet of parchment paper or plastic wrap on the counter and spoon the butter mixture in a line down the center of the sheet. Roll into a log about 1½ inches in diameter, twist the ends closed, and place in the refrigerator or freezer until needed. (The butter can be stored in the refrigerator for up to 2 weeks or in the freezer for up to 3 months. If frozen, defrost the butter in the refrigerator before using.)

Pork Burgers on Portobello Buns

Using portobello mushrooms in burgers is not new, but usually you see the mushrooms as the replacement for the protein. Forget that. Here, the portobellos are doubled up and used as delicious, messy, moist buns housing an equally flavorful pork-based burger. The flavors here work extremely well together and the mushrooms hold up well to any topping. Beware the mess though, as the buns and the patties both drip while you eat them. Wrap the burgers in napkins or roll up your sleeves and lean over your plate for maximum spill catching. These burgers taste great spread with Avocado Pesto Cream (page 53) and your favorite toppings, such as lettuce, tomato, and bacon.

YIELD: 4 SERVINGS

8 portobello mushrooms

1 Tbsp avocado oil or extra-virgin olive oil

Sea salt and fresh-cracked pepper

½ lb lean ground pastured pork

½ lb ground chicken

1 Tbsp Dijon mustard

2 tsp dried mixed herbs (oregano, basil, marjoram, etc.)

1 tsp liquid mesquite smoke (optional)

2 tsp coconut oil

1. Preheat the oven to 350°F. Line a baking sheet with parchment paper.

2. Remove the stems from the mushrooms and set aside (you can chop them finely and use in the burgers, or discard them). Brush the mushroom caps with the avocado oil and season with salt and pepper if desired.

3. Place the mushroom caps on the prepared baking sheet and bake for 10 to 15 minutes or until softened and slightly golden at edges. Cool to room temperature.

4. Mix the ground pork, ground chicken, mustard, herbs, liquid smoke (if using), chopped mushroom stems (if using), and 1 teaspoon of salt in a large bowl with your hands. Form the meat mixture into 4 patties slightly larger than your mushroom caps (they shrink a bit when cooked).

5. Melt the coconut oil in a large frying pan over medium heat, or preheat a grill. Cook the burgers for 5 to 7 minutes, flipping once. (The burgers are done when their juices run clear.)

6. Assemble the burgers and serve immediately.

Pork Tacos with Avocado Cream

There is nothing quite as satisfying as making your own tortillas. Their flavor is unrivaled by store-bought varieties; plus, you can make them any size you want. They have only three ingredients and once you make them you'll find it very hard to go back to the prepackaged kind. Here, homemade corn tortillas are filled with a spicy, meaty pork filling and topped with cooling avocado cream. It makes for an incomparable Mexican experience. Serve with your family's favorite toppings for a great hands-on dinner.

YIELD: 16 SMALL TACOS

Tortillas

2 cups masa harina

1½ cups water

½ tsp sea salt

Filling

2 tsp coconut oil

1½ lb lean ground pastured pork

½ lb extra-lean ground grass-fed beef or ground chicken

2 Tbsp chili powder

2 tsp ground cumin

2 tsp ground coriander

1 tsp sea salt

½ tsp garlic powder

2 tsp tapioca starch whisked into 1 Tbsp water

Avocado Cream

½ large avocado

¼ cup plain whole-milk yogurt

1 Tbsp lime juice

½ tsp ground cumin

¼ tsp sea salt

Optional Toppings

Chopped lettuce

Diced tomatoes

Shredded cheese

Salsa

1. For the tortillas: Mix all the ingredients in a small bowl until combined. Roll the dough into 16 small balls (about golf-ball size). Using a tortilla press covered in plastic wrap or wax paper, press each ball until about ⅛ inch thick. Alternatively, you can lay the dough between two sheets of wax paper and roll it out with a rolling pin.

2. Heat a small nonstick frying pan over medium-high heat. Place a tortilla in the pan and cook for about 1 minute on each side. Transfer to a covered bowl (I use a clean tea towel) to keep it warm and soft, and repeat with the remaining tortillas.

3. For the filling: In a large, heavy-bottomed frying pan, heat the coconut oil over medium heat.

4. Add the ground meat and cook until browned, 10 to 15 minutes, stirring to break up clumps. Add the chili powder, coriander, cumin, salt, and garlic powder and mix to combine. Cook for 5 to 7 more minutes, then remove from the heat and stir in the tapioca slurry.

5. For the avocado cream: Process all the ingredients in a blender or food processor until smooth. Transfer to a small bowl.

6. Lay the tortillas on plates, spoon some filling on each tortilla, and serve immediately, passing the toppings and avocado cream at the table.

Pulled Pork and Avocado Rice Bowls

There's nothing quite like the smell of pork roast simmering away in a slow cooker for hours and hours. Coming home to a meal that has practically cooked itself is a welcome treat in our house. Prep the ingredients for the roast the night before and turn it on first thing in the morning before leaving for school or work. Eight hours later, all you need to do is make the rice and cut the avocado and dinner is ready. This dish is great for dinner guests, leaving you plenty of time to catch up with old friends.

YIELD: 6–8 SERVINGS

4 tsp coconut oil

Sea salt and fresh-cracked pepper

1 (5-lb) boneless pastured pork butt or leg roast

⅓ cup Dijon mustard

½ cup white wine

4¾ cups water

2 sprigs fresh rosemary

3 cloves garlic, peeled

2 cups jasmine rice

1 large avocado, halved, pitted, and peeled

¼ cup plain nonfat Greek yogurt

2 Tbsp chopped sun-dried tomatoes

1½ Tbsp lemon juice

1. Heat 2 teaspoons of the oil in a large cast-iron frying pan over medium-high heat. Season the pork roast with salt and pepper and sear on all sides until golden brown. Transfer the roast to a slow cooker.

2. In a small bowl, whisk the white wine and mustard together and pour over the pork roast. Add ¾ cup of the water to the bottom of the slow cooker and toss in the garlic cloves and rosemary sprigs. Cover and cook on LOW for 8 hours or until fork-tender.

3. Thirty minutes before the roast is done, combine the remaining 4 cups water, rice, and remaining 2 teaspoons coconut oil in a medium saucepan and bring to a boil over high heat. Cover, lower the heat, and simmer for 15 minutes. Remove from the heat and let stand, covered, for 10 minutes.

4. In a small bowl, mash the avocado with a fork and stir in the yogurt, sun-dried tomatoes, lemon juice, and sea salt to taste.

5. When the pork is done, use two forks to pull the meat apart until shredded. (You can pull it directly in the crock with the liquid, which creates a beautifully moist dish.)

6. Fluff the rice with a fork, then spoon some into individual serving bowls. Top with pulled pork and mashed avocado, and serve.

Roasted Salmon with Creamy Avocado

Having grown up with a mother who was a professional salmon-fishing guide, I had my fair share of salmon as a child. We ate it in many, many different ways, from smoked and cured to barbecued, baked, and fried. In this iteration of roasted salmon (a dish I still make quite often in the summer), the fillet is coated in a thick and creamy cream cheese–based sauce and baked until medium-rare (the best way to serve salmon to retain its moist qualities). Serve this with or on top of salad or with roasted potatoes and grilled vegetables.

YIELD: 6–8 SERVINGS

4 ounces cream cheese, softened

1 large avocado, halved, pitted, and peeled

½ tsp grated lemon zest plus 3 Tbsp lemon juice

½ clove garlic, minced or grated

2 Tbsp capers

2 lb salmon fillets

1. Preheat the oven to 400°F. Line a baking sheet with aluminum foil.

2. Using a blender or an electric mixer, blend the cream cheese, avocado, garlic, and lemon zest and juice, until smooth. Stir in the capers.

3. Place the salmon fillets on the baking sheet skin side down. Spread the sauce over the fillets and cook for 10 to 15 minutes. (The salmon is done when the flesh is slightly firm and the juices just begin to turn white.) Serve immediately.

Variation: Brush the salmon fillets with 1 to 2 tablespoons of avocado oil and season with salt and pepper. Bake the salmon as directed and serve the avocado cream cheese sauce on the side.

Stuffed Peppers

Stuffed peppers are served all over the world in various forms, topped with cheese or sauces such as béchamel or chili. They can be a great way to serve a colorful and healthy dinner in a cute little vegetable package and can be made even healthier by choosing lighter toppings such as avocado. Use any color of pepper you desire and serve along with a side salad or steamed vegetables for a truly healthy meal.

YIELD: 6 SERVINGS

Peppers

1½ cups water

1 cup jasmine rice

3 tsp coconut oil

1½ tsp sea salt

6 bell peppers, halved lengthwise, stemmed, and seeded

½ sweet onion, chopped

¾ cup sliced white or cremini mushrooms

2 lb extra-lean ground grass-fed beef, ground chicken, or lean ground pastured pork

1 Tbsp chili powder

1 tsp dried oregano

1 tsp ground cumin

1 tsp ground coriander

3 Tbsp tomato paste

1 cup grated Parmesan or mozzarella cheese (optional)

Topping

1 large avocado, halved, pitted, and peeled

2 Tbsp lime juice

½ tsp ground cumin

¼ tsp sea salt

1. For the peppers: Preheat the oven to 400°F. Line a baking sheet with parchment paper or a silicone liner.

2. In a small saucepan, combine the water, rice, 2 teaspoons of the oil, and ½ teaspoon salt. Bring to a boil over high heat. Lower the heat, cover, and simmer for 15 minutes. Remove from the heat and let stand, covered, for 10 minutes.

3. In a large, heavy-bottomed frying pan, heat the remaining 1 teaspoon oil over medium heat. Add the onion and mushrooms and cook 10 to 15 minutes or until browned. Add the ground beef, chili powder, oregano, cumin, and coriander and cook for another 10 to 15 minutes or until the meat is cooked through.

4. Off the heat, add the rice and tomato paste to the meat mixture and stir to combine. Spoon into the pepper halves and place them on the baking sheet. Cover with aluminum foil and cook for 15 to 20 minutes. Remove the foil, top with the cheese (if using) and cook 10 minutes more.

5. For the topping: In a small bowl, mash the avocado with a fork and stir in the lime juice, cumin, and salt. Spoon the avocado mixture over the peppers and serve.

Desserts and Baked Goods

Avocado-Lime Ice Pops

Avocado is often paired with lime, and for good reason. Here, the tangy lime plays an important role in perking up the subtle creaminess of the avocado. Flavored with a hint of vanilla and coconut, these ice pops are reminiscent of tropical climes. The xanthan gum in this recipe acts as a thickener and also helps keep the ice pops from becoming rock-hard. If you can't find xanthan gum, the ice pops will still taste fine, but they may be slightly harder to eat. Coconut cream is available in most grocery stores in the same place you would find coconut milk. Like coconut milk, it is unsweetened, but it's higher in fat and thicker—perfect for use in frozen desserts.

YIELD: 4 LARGE ICE POPS

¾ cup coconut cream

½ large avocado

3 Tbsp raw honey

2 tsp grated lime zest plus 3 Tbsp lime juice

1 tsp vanilla extract

Pinch sea salt

½ tsp xanthan gum

1. Process the coconut cream, avocado, honey, lime zest and juice, vanilla, and salt in a blender or food processor until smooth.

2. Add the xanthan gum and process to blend.

3. Pour into an ice pop mold and freeze for a minimum of 8 hours.

4. Remove from the ice pop mold by running the mold under warm water and sliding the ice pops out.

Avocado Ice Cream

With their cool color and lush texture, avocados lend themselves perfectly to making rich, creamy, ice cream perfect for pairing with fresh fruits like mangoes, pineapples, peaches, nectarines, and strawberries. You can also serve this ice cream with chocolate sauce, on fruit pies, or all by itself straight out of the container with a spoon. No one is judging you here. Coconut cream is available in most grocery stores in the same place you would find regular coconut milk. Like coconut milk, it is unsweetened, but it's higher in fat and thicker—perfect for use in frozen desserts.

YIELD: 7 CUPS

¼ cup honey

¼ cup coconut sugar or organic unrefined
   cane sugar

3 Tbsp lime juice

1 Tbsp vanilla extract

Pinch sea salt

2 avocados, halved, pitted, and peeled

1 (14-oz) can full-fat coconut milk

1 (14-oz) can coconut cream

½ –1 tsp liquid stevia (optional)

1. In a small saucepan over medium-low heat, mix the honey, coconut sugar, lime juice, vanilla, and salt until the sugar is dissolved.

2. In a blender or food processor, process the avocados with the coconut milk and coconut cream until smooth. Add the honey-lime mixture and blend again to mix. Taste the mixture and add stevia if desired.

3. Place the mixture in an ice cream maker and follow the manufacturer's instructions. If you don't have an ice cream machine, pour the mixture into a shallow metal container (plastic will do in a pinch) and place in the freezer. Stir with a spoon or spatula every 30 minutes or so until completely frozen (4 to 6 hours).

4. Remove the ice cream from the freezer and let sit at room temperature for 30 minutes to soften slightly before serving. (The ice cream will last up to 3 weeks in the freezer.)

Avocado Mousse

Light and fluffy, this dessert is a refreshing blend of avocados and lime, sweetened with honey and served in tall glasses. It makes for a quick and healthy dessert and adds a touch of elegance to any meal. It can be made up to 4 hours in advance and stores well, covered, in the refrigerator. For the best flavor, serve the mousse the same day you make it.

YIELD: 4 SERVINGS

1 large avocado, halved, pitted, and peeled

3 Tbsp lime juice

3 Tbsp honey

1 Tbsp vanilla extract

1 cup plus 2 Tbsp heavy cream

1. Process the avocado, lime juice, honey, vanilla, and 2 tablespoons of the cream in a blender or food processor until smooth.

2. In a large bowl with an electric mixer, whip the remaining 1 cup cream until stiff. Fold in the avocado mixture and place in bowls or tall glasses.

3. Cover and refrigerate for 2 to 4 hours before serving.

Avocado Rice Pudding

I was never a big fan of rice pudding when I was a kid; I always thought of it as a grandmotherly kind of dessert. It was usually dotted with raisins (not my favorite) and served for dessert at other people's houses. It was not until I had tried making it myself as an adult that I truly appreciated its intricate textures and delicate flavors. Done right, rice pudding can be a treat for anyone in the family. Here, it is paired with spices and coconut milk for an exotic touch.

YIELD: 4 SERVINGS

1 large avocado, halved, pitted, and peeled

1½ cups canned full-fat coconut milk

1 cup water

3 Tbsp honey

1 Tbsp vanilla extract

2 Tbsp butter or coconut oil

1 cup short-grain white rice (such as Arborio)

½ tsp ground cinnamon

¼ tsp ground nutmeg

⅛ tsp ground cardamom

1. Process the avocado, coconut milk, water, honey, and vanilla in a blender or food processor until smooth.

2. In a medium saucepan, heat the butter over medium heat. Add the rice, cinnamon, nutmeg, and cardamom and stir to coat.

3. Stir in the blended avocado mixture and bring to a boil over high heat. Lower the heat, cover, and simmer, stirring often until the rice is tender and the liquid is absorbed, about 25 minutes.

4. Serve warm or cover and refrigerate to serve cool.

Chocolate Avocado Pudding

One of my favorite ways to eat avocado is with chocolate. The first time I ever heard of this combination I thought the chef was crazy and that it would be terrible. Boy, was I wrong! With a generous half cup of cocoa providing plenty of chocolate flavor, the avocado is undetectable in this pudding except for its smooth, creamy texture. The key to using avocado in puddings is to make sure you completely puree the flesh, so that there are no undesirable lumps of avocado in your pudding.

YIELD: 4 CUPS

2 large avocados, halved, pitted, and peeled

1 cup canned full-fat coconut milk

½ cup cocoa powder

⅓ cup honey or maple syrup

2 tsp vanilla extract

1 tsp instant coffee powder

¼ tsp sea salt

1. Process all the ingredients in a blender or food processor until completely smooth, scraping down the sides of the bowl as needed.

2. Pour the pudding into a bowl or other dish and refrigerate for 1 to 2 hours.

3. Stir the refrigerated pudding, spoon into serving dishes, and serve.

Avocado Truffles

With a gooey green center and a luscious dark chocolate coating, these avocado truffles make a fun-filled dessert that is perfect for gatherings. Although they seem like they might be complicated, they are actually quite simple to make. Give them as gifts over the holidays and watch in delight as your friends and family bite into them. With their mysterious green centers, most people cannot tell what they are made from. For a vegan variation, use maple syrup or agave nectar in place of the honey.

YIELD: 30–35 TRUFFLES

Truffles

2 oz cacao butter

3 Tbsp honey

3 Tbsp coconut butter

2 Tbsp coconut oil

1 avocado, pureed smooth

3 Tbsp heavy cream or canned full-fat coconut milk

1 tsp grated lime zest plus 1 Tbsp lime juice

Seeds of 1 vanilla bean

Coating

7 oz bittersweet chocolate, roughly chopped

3 Tbsp honey

2 Tbsp coconut oil

2 tsp vanilla extract

1. For the truffles: In a double boiler, combine the cacao butter, honey, coconut butter, and coconut oil and heat over medium heat until completely melted. (You can also use a small metal bowl set over a saucepan of simmering water, but don't allow the bowl to touch the water.)

2. In a blender or food processor, process the avocado, heavy cream, lime zest and juice, and vanilla seeds until smooth. Pour the melted cacao butter mixture into the avocado mixture and blend until smooth. Transfer to a bowl, cover, and refrigerate until firm, 3 to 4 hours.

3. Line a baking sheet with parchment paper. Using a melon baller or spoons, scoop the avocado mixture into ¾-inch balls (about 1½ teaspoons each). (You can roll them in your hand until perfectly round, though be mindful that they will begin to soften and melt quickly.) Place the balls on the prepared baking sheet and freeze until hard.

4. For the coating: In a double boiler, combine the chocolate, honey, coconut oil, and vanilla and heat over medium heat, stirring occasionally, until completely melted. (If you use a metal bowl and saucepan, be sure not to let the bowl touch the simmering water.) Place the frozen avocado balls in the chocolate one at a time, and roll until covered. Remove with spoons and place back on the baking sheet.

5. Chill the truffles in the refrigerator until the coating is firm. Serve chilled. (The truffles may be stored in an airtight container in the refrigerator for up to 1 week.)

Morning Glory Muffins

Morning glory muffins are a breakfast classic made with apples, grated carrots, spices, and raisins. Usually they are full of vegetable oils, white flour, and sugar and are not something I would call healthy. Here, unhealthy fats are replaced completely with avocado and nonfat Greek yogurt, making for a great alternative. These freeze and defrost very well and make perfect handheld snacks for little ones.

YIELD: 12 MUFFINS

⅔ cup coconut flour, sifted

½ cup coconut sugar or organic unrefined cane sugar

⅓ cup tapioca flour

2 tsp baking soda

2 tsp ground cinnamon

½ tsp ground nutmeg

½ tsp sea salt

1 firm apple (Granny Smith, Honey Crisp, or Pink Lady work best), peeled, cored, and grated

1 cup grated peeled carrot

½ cup raisins (optional)

½ large avocado

⅓ cup plain nonfat Greek yogurt

4 pastured eggs

2 tsp apple cider vinegar

2 tsp vanilla extract

1. Preheat the oven to 350°F. Line a muffin tin with paper liners.

2. In a large bowl, whisk together the coconut flour, sugar, tapioca flour, baking soda, cinnamon, nutmeg, and salt. Stir in the apple, carrot, and raisins (if using).

3. In a blender or food processor, process the avocado with the yogurt until very smooth. Add the eggs, vinegar, and vanilla and process again.

4. Pour the wet ingredients into the dry and stir to combine. Divide the batter evenly into the lined muffin cups and bake for 25 to 30 minutes. The muffins are done when a toothpick inserted into the center comes out clean

5. Cool the muffins in the tin for 10 minutes, then remove the muffins and cool completely on a wire rack before serving. (The muffins can be stored in an airtight container at room temperature for up to 2 days, in the refrigerator for up to 1 week, or in the freezer for up to 6 weeks).

Vanilla Oat Muffins

These muffins are the perfect blank slate for any additions you might normally see in a muffin. They are perfect with fresh, dried, or frozen fruit, nuts, or even chocolate chips. They freeze and defrost very well and are delicious served warm with a bit of butter or jam.

YIELD: 8 MUFFINS

1½ cups gluten-free oat flour*

⅓ cup coconut flour

⅓ cup tapioca or arrowroot flour

¼ cup coconut sugar

2 tsp baking powder

½ tsp ground cinnamon

½ tsp sea salt

1 cup fresh, frozen or dried fruit, ¾ cup chopped nuts, or ½ cup semisweet chocolate chips (optional)

2 pastured eggs

⅓ cup plain nonfat Greek yogurt

⅓ cup almond milk or other nondairy milk

¼ cup avocado oil

¼ cup maple syrup

2 tsp apple cider vinegar

1 Tbsp vanilla extract

Seeds from 1 vanilla bean

1. Preheat the oven to 350°F. Line eight cups in a muffin tin with paper liners.

2. In a medium bowl, whisk together the flours, sugar, baking powder, cinnamon, and salt. Stir in the fruit, nuts, or chocolate chips (if using).

3. In a large bowl, whisk the eggs. Add the yogurt, almond milk, avocado oil, maple syrup, vinegar, vanilla extract, vanilla seeds and stir to combine.

4. Pour the dry ingredients into the wet ingredients and stir until just combined. Divide the batter evenly into the lined muffin cups and bake for 22 to 25 minutes. The muffins are done when a toothpick inserted into the center comes out clean.

5. Cool the muffins in the tin for 10 minutes, then remove the muffins and cool completely on a wire rack before serving. (The muffins can be stored in an airtight container at room temperature for up to 2 days, in the refrigerator for up to 1 week, or in the freezer for up to 6 weeks).

Notes: To make your own oat flour, process slightly more quick oats than the recipe calls for (1 cup oats yields about ¾ cup oat flour) in a coffee grinder or food processor until very fine.

Avocado Brownies

Chocolate and avocados were made for each other. The creamy, buttery consistency of the avocado blends perfectly with the bitterness of the chocolate in baked goods like cakes, brownies, and cookies. These brownies are gluten-free, grain-free, and dairy-free but are still quite dense and flavorful with the avocado completely replacing any butter or oil you would normally use. Keep in mind they are lower in sugar than your standard brownie so they won't have that crackled top, but nobody misses that in my house when I put these out on the table! It is essential to the texture of the brownies (and for visual appeal) that there be no lumps in the avocado puree, so be sure to process accordingly.

YIELD: 9–12 BROWNIES

2 cups blanched almond meal/flour

½ cup cocoa powder

3 Tbsp coconut flour

1 tsp baking soda

½ tsp sea salt

½ cup coconut sugar

½ cup pureed avocado (about ¾ large avocado)

2 pastured eggs

2 tsp vanilla extract

¼ cup maple syrup

½ cup semisweet chocolate chips (optional)

1. Preheat the oven to 325°F. Grease an 8 x 8-inch pan with coconut oil or butter.

2. In a medium bowl, whisk together the almond meal, cocoa, coconut flour, baking soda, and salt.

3. In a separate bowl, whisk the coconut sugar with the pureed avocado. Add the eggs one at a time, beating with the whisk between additions. Whisk in the vanilla and maple syrup.

4. Pour the dry ingredients into the wet ingredients and stir to combine. Stir in the chocolate chips (if using). Pour the batter into the prepared pan and bake for 25 minutes. The brownies are done when the edges begin to pull away from the sides of the pan and the center is soft to the touch but not wet.

5. Cool in the pan for at least 20 minutes before serving. The texture improves as the brownies cool. (The brownies can be stored in an airtight container at room temperature for up to 4 days.)

Vanilla-Lemon Snack Cake

Not all cakes are meant to be frosted or stacked; some are humble and unassuming, perfect for coffee with friends or a casual weekend brunch. This cake, topped with a tart lemon glaze, tastes great with coffee or tea, after a light meal, or simply on its own as a snack. This cake is quite dense and hearty, similar to baked oatmeal in texture, and does not rise as far as most other cakes.

YIELD: ONE 9-INCH CAKE

Cake

⅔ cup organic unrefined cane sugar

½ cup pureed avocado (about ¾ large avocado)

½ cup salted butter, at room temperature

3 pastured eggs

2 Tbsp vanilla extract

½ cup plain nonfat Greek yogurt

¼ cup unsweetened almond milk or other nut milk

1 tsp grated lemon zest plus 3 Tbsp lemon juice

1¼ cups gluten-free oat flour*

⅔ cup coconut flour, sifted

⅓ cup tapioca flour

¼ cup ground golden flaxseeds

2 tsp baking powder

½ tsp sea salt

Glaze

1 tsp grated lemon zest plus 9 Tbsp lemon juice (about 3 lemons)

⅔ cup organic unrefined cane sugar

Seeds of 1 vanilla bean or 2 tsp vanilla extract

1. Preheat the oven to 350°F. Grease a 9-inch springform pan.

2. For the cake: In a large bowl with an electric mixer, cream the sugar, pureed avocado, and butter together.

3. Beat in the eggs one at a time, completely incorporating one before adding the next. Beat in the vanilla, yogurt, milk, and lemon zest and juice.

4. In a separate large bowl, whisk together the oat flour, coconut flour, tapioca flour, flaxseeds, baking powder, and salt until well blended.

5. Pour the wet ingredients into the dry ingredients and stir to combine. Pour into the prepared pan and bake until a toothpick inserted in the center comes out clean, 35 to 40 minutes.

6. For the glaze: In a small saucepan, combine all the ingredients and bring to a boil over high heat. Lower the heat and simmer for 20 to 25 minutes. Strain while hot, if desired, to remove the lemon zest. Cool completely, then pour over the cake and serve. (The cake will keep at room temperature for up to 1 week.)

Notes: To make your own oat flour, blend slightly more quick oats than the recipe calls for (1 cup oats yields about ¾ cup oat flour) in a coffee grinder or food processor until very fine.

Chocolate Fudge Cake

The thick and creamy avocado gives this cake a wonderfully rich and fudge-like consistency. Because of the denseness of this cake, don't expect it to rise too far; it's more like a flourless cake, even though it contains flour. Once you cover it with the creamy Chocolate Fudge Frosting, no one will ever know there's a green monster lurking in there. Make sure the avocado puree is absolutely smooth—no lumps!

YIELD: ONE 9-INCH LAYER CAKE

¾ cup coconut flour

¾ cup cocoa powder

½ cup tapioca flour

2 tsp baking powder

1 tsp sea salt

½ tsp ground cinnamon

6 pastured eggs, separated

1 cup pureed avocado (about 1¼ large avocados)

1 cup strong brewed coffee, room temperature

⅔ cup maple syrup or honey

1 Tbsp vanilla extract

2 tsp aged balsamic vinegar or apple cider vinegar

1 tsp cream of tartar

3 cups Chocolate Fudge Frosting (page 131)

1. Preheat the oven to 325°F. Grease two 9-inch round pans. Line the bottoms of the pans with parchment paper, then grease the paper.

2. In a small bowl, whisk together the coconut flour, cocoa, tapioca flour, baking powder, salt, and cinnamon.

3. In a large bowl, whisk together the egg yolks, pureed avocado, coffee, maple syrup, vanilla, and vinegar.

4. In another large bowl with an electric mixer, beat the egg whites until foamy. Add the cream of tartar and beat again until stiff peaks form.

5. Mix the dry ingredients into the wet and then fold the egg whites into the batter.

6. Divide the batter evenly between the prepared pans and bake until set, about 35 minutes. The cakes are done when their tops spring back when pressed lightly. Transfer the cakes to a wire cooling rack and cool in the pans for 20 minutes. Gently run a small knife around the pan edges and quickly turn the cakes out onto the wire rack. Cool completely, then frost with the Chocolate Fudge Frosting and serve.

Chocolate Fudge Frosting

This frosting might just be one of the best chocolate frostings out there—super-chocolaty, fudgelike consistency, pipeable, vegan, paleo, and gluten-free too! It's lower in fat than just about every frosting out there; plus, it's super-simple to make and looks just like any old chocolate frosting. Use this wonderful concoction anywhere you would use a buttercream frosting.

YIELD: ABOUT 3 CUPS

2 cups pureed avocado (about 2½ large avocados)

8 soft medjool dates, pitted

4 oz semisweet chocolate, roughly chopped

¼ cup maple syrup or honey

3 Tbsp coconut oil

1 Tbsp vanilla extract

⅓ cup cocoa powder

1. Process the avocados and dates in a blender or food processor until smooth. Scrape down the sides of the bowl as needed.

2. In a double boiler, melt the chocolate over medium heat. (You can also use a small metal bowl set over a saucepan of simmering water, but don't allow the bowl to touch the water.) Stir in the maple syrup, coconut oil, and vanilla.

3. Combine the melted chocolate mixture with the avocado mixture in the blender or food processor and process until smooth. Add the cocoa and process again.

4. Place the mixture in the refrigerator for 2 to 3 hours to firm up. Remove from the refrigerator and, using an electric mixer, beat until fluffy.

5. Now frost your cake, or cupcakes, or toast or . . .

Mini Avocado Cheesecakes

Cheesecake has always been something I love to eat, but hate to cook. It's fickle, finicky, and tends to need handling with extreme caution and care. Usually there is some sort of water bath or other delicate treatment needed and often I've resorted to wrapping the pan in an aluminum foil robe as well. This recipe is a little more beginner-friendly because of the size of the cakes themselves. The avocado creates a wonderful green tinge that is not too overwhelming for those who might balk at eating a green cake. Top these little cakes with a generous scoop of whipped cream and you have yourself a perfectly portioned dessert for any occasion.

YIELD: 6 SERVINGS

Crusts

1¼ cups blanched almond meal/flour

3 Tbsp unsalted butter, softened

2 Tbsp organic unrefined cane sugar

¼ tsp sea salt

Filling

8 oz light cream cheese

¾ cup pureed avocado (about 1 large avocado)

1 pastured egg

2 tsp vanilla extract

½ tsp grated lime zest plus 3 Tbsp lime juice (about 2 large limes)

3 Tbsp honey

Topping

1 cup heavy cream

1 Tbsp honey

1 tsp vanilla extract

1. Preheat the oven to 350°F. Line a jumbo muffin tin (with six cups) with paper liners.

2. For the crusts: In a large bowl, using a fork, mix all the ingredients together until completely incorporated. Divide into the muffin cups and press into the liners. (You can use the bottom of a small spice jar to get an even pressure when pressing down.)

3. Bake the crusts for 15 minutes. Remove from the oven and cool for at least 10 minutes. Reduce the oven temperature to 300°F.

4. For the filling: In a blender, food processor, or a large bowl with an electric mixer, blend all the ingredients together until smooth. Pour into the cooled crusts and bake for 22 to 25 minutes. Turn the oven off, prop the oven door open, and leave the cakes in for another 10 minutes. (The cheesecakes should be slightly jiggly when shaken but should not be soupy. Cracks and overbrowned edges can mean they've been overcooked. But this is not a huge concern as the avocado keeps this cheesecake very moist.)

5. Cool in the tin on a wire rack, then remove the cheesecakes from the tin.

6. For the topping: In a bowl with an electric mixer, beat all the ingredients until thick. Pipe or spoon the whipped cream onto the cooled cheesecakes and serve.

Index

MEASUREMENT CONVERSION TABLES

The following tables provide equivalents for U.S., metric, and Imperial (U.K.) units of measure.
Values have been rounded up or down to the nearest whole number.

VOLUME

U.S.	METRIC
1 teaspoon	5 milliliters
1 tablespoon	15 milliliters
¼ cup	59 milliliters
⅓ cup	79 milliliters
½ cup	118 milliliters
¾ cup	177 milliliters
1 cup	237 milliliters
4 cups (1 quart)	.95 liter
1.06 quarts	1 liter
4 quarts (1 gallon)	3.8 liters

WEIGHT

OUNCES	GRAMS
½	14
1	28
8	227
12	340
16 (1 pound)	454

COOKING TEMPERATURE/DEGREES

To convert Fahrenheit to Celsius,
subtract 32 degrees from the Fahrenheit
temperature, then divide the result by
1.8 to find the Celsius equivalent.

Acknowledgments

Thanks to The Countryman Press, Ann Treistman, Jill Browning, Kermit Hummel, and everyone else who helped me get this book into your hands. I'd also like to thank my friends and family, who have supported my dreams for all these years and stuck by my side through the good and the bad. I may not have always taken your criticisms as well as you might have hoped, but I think after this book I may have changed my tune. Writing a book (or two!) has always been my dream, and without all of you, it would never have been possible. Thank you.